HOW TO DRESS
AN OLD-FASHIONED
DOLL

BY

MARY H. MORGAN

with 57 Illustrations

DOVER PUBLICATIONS, INC.

NEW YORK

Published in Canada by General Publishing Company, Ltd., 30 Lesmill Road, Don Mills, Toronto, Ontario.
Published in the United Kingdom by Constable and Company, Ltd., 10 Orange Street, London WC 2.

This Dover edition, first published in 1973, is an unabridged and unaltered republication of the work originally published by Henry Altemus Company, Philadelphia, in 1908 under the title *How to Dress a Doll*.

International Standard Book Number: 0-486-22912-2
Library of Congress Catalog Card Number: 72-93612

Manufactured in the United States of America
Dover Publications, Inc.
180 Varick Street
New York, N. Y. 10014

FOREWORD

TO YOUNG DRESSMAKERS

Little girl mothers have almost as much trouble as grown-up mothers about their children's clothes. It would never do if their dollies were not stylishly dressed; yet how to manage it is the bother. Mothers, big sisters and nurses are usually too busy to make lots of dainty underclothes, dresses, coats and hats for their doll family, and there do not seem to be many doll dressmakers and milliners.

This book will help you to get rid of that bother. It will show you how to have your dollies beautifully dressed without troubling big people or costing much money. How will it do it? By teaching you to make your dollies' clothes.

Look over the pages and see the interesting pictures. Here are clothes to be made for each member of your doll family — long dresses, coats, and caps for the wee baby; dainty underclothes, school frocks, and outdoor wraps for the older doll; an apron and a nice kimono for the mamma doll to lounge in. Better yet, there are a fine gown for birthday parties and quaint costumes if any of the dolls should be invited to a fancy dress affair.

The patterns are simple and easy for you to cut out and make, but you must follow the directions exactly. The small pictures show you how to work different stitches to trim your doll frocks, and also make plainer the various steps in sewing.

Of course, you will want to start on all these fine clothes at once; but that will never do unless you already know how to sew nicely. The pretty patterns would be quite spoiled by big stitches and crooked seams.

So, before you learn to cut out and make the infant's dress or any of the others, we will have a few lessons on some things all good dressmakers must know. Every girl, nowadays, wants to be a fine needlewoman, and the best way to become one is to sew your doll's clothes just as neatly as possible. Then, when you are grown up you can make yourself **lovely blouses and frocks.**

CHAPTER I

GENERAL SEWING HINTS

Correct Position for Sewing

Never sit on too high a chair; the feet should rest comfortably on the floor.

Sit so the end of the spine rests against the back of the chair. This will keep the body straight and prevent stooping or bending of the neck.

Hold the work up to you; do not lean over to it. Always keep the chest up and do not let the head droop forward, for it will cause headache.

The sewing should never be held close to the eyes, as it causes squinting and eye-strain.

Never rest the arm on chair or table when sewing, but keep the elbow close to the body, moving the wrist only.

Always sit with the light falling over the left shoulder. Never face the light or sew with the sun shining on the work.

MAKING PREPARATION

Always have clean hands before beginning to sew. If white work is to be done wear an apron or lay a towel or big handkerchief on the lap to keep the work clean.

Have a work-bag beside you holding pins, thimble, scissors, needles, thread and sewing-silk, an emery, a tape-measure or foot-rule, and a notched card for measuring hems.

Fold up your work neatly each time you are through with it; never jam it roughly into the work bag. Creased and rumpled materials are hard to sew.

THIMBLE EXERCISE

To sew without a thimble hurts the finger and prevents fast work. Wear it on the middle finger of the right hand. It should fit snugly but not pinch.

Practice the thimble motion by holding the thumb of the right hand from you almost at right angles and strike the under part of the first joint of it with the end of the thimble. Bend the two joints of the thimble finger slightly and work from the knuckle. This will give you the correct position of the finger, and should be repeated until the motion becomes natural.

Holding the finger bent correctly, keep the arm steady and move the wrist half-way round, from right to left, as if holding an imaginary needle.

Next take a good-sized needle and place it over the end of the thumb of the right hand, about a quarter of an inch from the point, holding it firmly with the first finger a little below the tip. Repeat the thimble-striking motions, but hit the end of the needle.

Hold a strip of stiff, white paper between the thumb and first finger of the left hand, keeping it firm between the third and fourth fingers. Holding the needle and thimble as directed, make a stitch in the paper. Push the needle through with the thimble until the eye is almost reached, then lift the hand and pull the point of the needle through with the thumb and first finger.

Make these stitches again and again, at first anywhere on the paper; later try to keep them in a straight line with the holes even distances apart.

Practice the paper-stitches with a zephyr

needle at first, gradually with smaller ones until the tiniest is reached. Not until then should thread be used.

SCISSORS AND HOW TO USE THEM

Use sharp scissors about five inches long, of the best steel. Also have a pair for button-holes and quite small pointed ones for cutting scallops or ripping.

Slip the thumb of the right hand through the broader hole and the second and third fingers through the other one, letting the scissors rest on the first finger for guidance and support. Open and shut them often.

Put the blunt blade of the scissors down on a table, with the thumb up, and practice open-ing and shutting the blades. Later, push the scissors away from you toward the back of the table, as if cutting along a line. Keep the blunt point on the table as it is done.

Practice cutting from right to left on the table in the same way.

Next practice cutting ruled paper, first fol-lowing the lines, then cutting between and across them. Later, circles, stars and other figures can be drawn on plain paper and be cut out.

Lastly, different sized squares may be measured with a ruler, marked with a pencil and cut along the lines. To be sure they are exact, draw two diagonal lines from corner to corner so they cross in the center.

With this practice it will be easy to cut out the patches, and later the patterns, without assistance.

Never use scissors that have grown too dull to cut well, or the edges of the material will be jagged.

Needles and Their Management

Ordinary sewing needles are of three kinds —"sharps," "betweens" and "ground-downs." "Sharps" are the ones most people use when sewing. "Betweens" are shorter, but if one gets used to them one will like them much better and can do faster work. "Ground-downs" are very tiny and are not often used except for very fine work.

Needles are numbered from 1 to 12; Number 1 being the coarsest. The finer the material the finer should be the needle.

There are also crewel, darning and zephyr needles which have long eyes so as to hold heavier threads.

To thread a needle, hold it in the right hand partly resting on the tip of the second finger, the eye about an eighth of an inch above the first finger, pressed tight by the thumb. [Fig. 1.]

Hold the thread between the thumb and first finger of the left hand about a quarter of

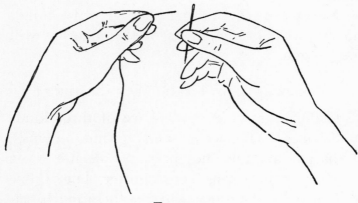

FIGURE 1

an inch from the end, steadying it by the other fingers.

To get the thread through the eye, rest the first joint of the left-hand thumb against that of the right-hand thumb and press hard, guiding the thread through the eye at the same time.

As soon as the point can be seen on the other side of the eye, slip the needle between

the thumb and first finger of the left hand
and pull the thread through with the tips
of the thumb and first finger of the right
hand.

Practice needle-threading until it can be done
quickly.   First use coarse-eyed needles and fine

FIGURE 2

thread, gradually reaching proper sizes.
Crewel needles are threaded by folding back
the end of the thread and pushing it through
doubled.

The position of the needle for sewing is between the thumb and first finger of the right

hand, about a quarter of an inch from the point, with the end pressed against the end of the thimble.   [Fig. 2.]

Never use a rusty, bent needle, nor one too large for the thread nor so coarse that it makes holes in the material.

Always have an emery in the sewing-basket to run the needle through when it gets sticky. If thread is not bitten and the hands are kept clean, the needles will be easier to work with.

The Thread

Plain sewing on cotton materials is done with basting cotton and other cotton threads, which are numbered from 1 to 200, the lower numbers being the coarsest.

For wool or silk fabrics sewing silk is used; it is numbered by letters from "AA" to "E," the coarsest being "E."   There is also a but tonhole twist of silk in different letters from "A" to "E."

Scallops, catch-stitching and feather-stitching are done in mercerized cottons which have a lustre like silk but are cheaper and wash better.

Basting may be done with a coarse white

basting cotton, though many people prefer using a Number 40. Never baste with silk; it is wasteful.

Do not use too long a thread, as it twists, tangles and gets rough and thin. The distance from shoulder to shoulder is about the right length.

Always put through the eye of the needle the end of the thread that is not broken from the spool. This prevents tangling and knots. To make sure of doing it, the needle may be threaded before the thread is cut from the spool.

A Number 7 needle usually takes 40 to 50 thread; a Number 8 needle, 60 to 80 thread; a Number 9 needle, 90 to 110 thread. Use the finer needles for all cottons over 110. If a thread is in a needle too fine for it, it will stick and must be jerked through the material.

Never use a coarse needle and thread on stiff silks, even for basting, as they leave holes in the material.

Never wet the end of the thread to go through the eye, but twist it to a point between the thumb and first finger of the right hand.

Knots

A knot should be round, small, with the end entirely fastened in.

To make it, hold the thread about two inches from the end, between the thumb and first finger of the right hand, and under the third and little finger to make it firm [Fig. 3]. Put

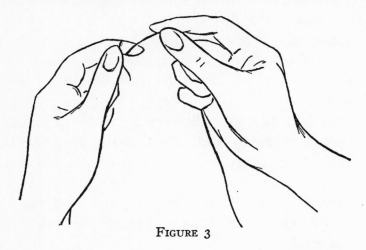

FIGURE 3

the thread around the tip of the first finger of the left hand with the end next to the thumb and below the loop. With the tip of the thumb twist this thread over the loop several times until it works off the finger, when it is held firm on the thumb while the twist is drawn down tight with the nail of the second finger.

Making a knot is difficult for most children and should be practiced over and over again.

Tape Measure and Hem Marker

Learn the use of a tape measure or foot rule, and mark off inches, half inches, quarter inches and less on a piece of paper. Also learn to measure a yard and its divisions, a half, a quarter, eighth and sixteenth of a yard.

A narrow, stiff piece of cardboard should have notches marked on it at intervals to measure hems and turn-downs of different widths.

Lay the paper flat on the table, keeping it firm with the second finger of the right hand, and hold the measure, notched side down, so the end comes to the edge of the paper. Measure the right depth, crease with the thumb of the right hand, shove the measure along with the left one and at the same time fold over more of the turn-down.

The edge of the paper must be even, or else straight folds cannot be made.

Practice all widths of turn-downs on paper; also practice folding over and measuring a second time as if for a hem.

Warp, Woof and Selvage

Every material has two kinds of threads—those that run up and down and those that run across. The threads that run up and down, or the lengthwise of the material, are called the warp; those that run across the material, from one selvage to the other, are called the woof.

A bias cut is made diagonally across the warp and woof threads. To get it, fold the material so the woof, or cross-threads, lie along the warp, or lengthwise threads. Cut through the crease thus made. This slanting edge is used as a guide for measuring bias strips for facing or binding. Practice cutting bias strips with squares of paper, folding the lower edge so it lies along the side edge; then cut through the crease.

"Selvage" means the woven or finished edge to the material.

CHAPTER II

SOME SIMPLE STITCHES

BASTING

Basting is sewing with large stitches to prepare the work for the real sewing with small stitches. For ordinary basting, make the stitches an inch long with an eighth of an inch space between. Basting is most important, for the straighter the basting the more even will be the finished work. Always use white basting cotton and begin with a knot on the *right* side of the garment. A knot is used because basting threads are always pulled out. The knot is put on the right side so as to be more easily seen.

RUNNING

Running-stitches are much the same as basting stitches, only much smaller. The space between is equal. The running-stitch is used for seams where not much strength is necessary; also for gathering and for tucks.

BINDING

A binding is used to cover raw edges. It is sometimes of a contrasting color for ornamentation. It is generally a narrow piece of the material cut on the bias. It is basted to the edge, right side to right side. Sew just below the line of basting, fold over on the wrong side, turn in the edge of the bias piece and hem so the work does not show on the right side.

FACING

A facing is used instead of a hem. It is either cut on the bias or is shaped to the place to be faced. It is basted and sewed with right side to right side and then is turned over and basted on the edge. Lastly, turn in the upper edge and hem down.

SEAMING

Seaming is the joining together of two separate pieces. First, baste the edges together; then make the seam a little below the basting with a running- and a back-stitch. That means, take two stitches forward and then go back one stitch, being careful to put the needle exactly where the previous stitch went in. When you get to the end of the seam, take out the bastings, and the edges are ready to overcast. When overcasting, hold the work firmly between the thumb and first finger of the left hand, the hand being always over the work.

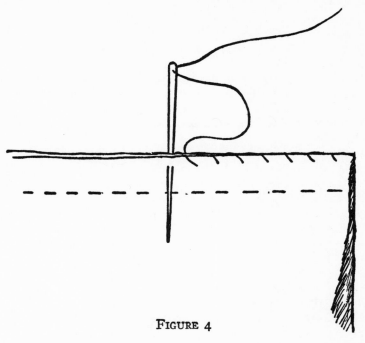

FIGURE 4

Never in overcasting, or overhanding, hold the work around the first finger. Put the needle in straight, at right angles to the seam, with the point toward you. This makes a slanting stitch. [Fig. 4.] To have the overcasting quite perfect, the stitches must be not only at equal distances, but of equal depth.

The difference between overcasting and overhanding is that overhanding is the real sewing of the seam itself; while overcasting is only used to keep raw edges on a seam already sewed, from fraying. Overhanding is simply

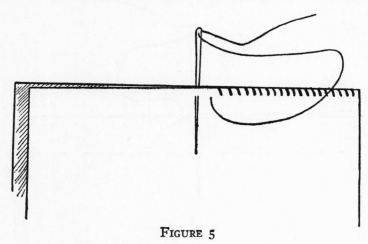

FIGURE 5

sewing over-and-over, close to the edge, with very small stitches. [Fig. 5.]

THE FELLED SEAM

Next comes the felled seam. This is made by sewing the raw edges together with a running and a back-stitch, one edge an eighth of an

inch below the other. Next, turn the wide edge
over the narrow one and hem down neatly to
make a flat seam. The stitches should be
small and perfectly even. [Fig. 6.]

When two bias edges come together they
should always be felled.

The French fell is much easier to make.

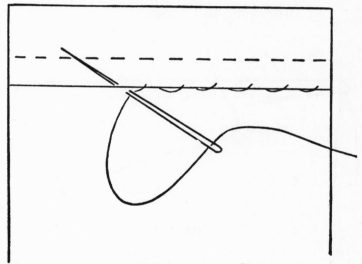

FIGURE 6

Sew the edges together with the narrowest possible seam, first on the right side of the
garment. Then turn, and on the wrong side
make a seam just large enough to cover the
raw edges of the other seam. [Fig. 7.]

Always cut the thread. Never under any circumstances break it, for it is almost sure to cause trouble. The beginning and ending of sewing are very important, and great care should be taken to do both right. Begin with a small knot, if it can be concealed; otherwise, with two or three over-and-over stitches. End

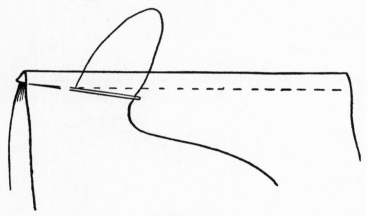

FIGURE 7

also with a few over-and-over stitches to prevent the work from ripping.

In sewing a long seam it is sometimes difficult to have the ends come out even. To prevent this unevenness, begin to sew from one end to the middle; then from the other end to meet it.

Hemming

Hemming is finishing a piece of work by folding over the raw edge twice, and then sewing down the fold. The first fold is made as narrow as possible [Fig. 8], and must be exact, for the evenness of the hem depends upon the first fold. For a very narrow hem,

Figure 8

the second turn-over is just the same width as the first fold.

For a wider hem, use a notched card. Measure for the width of hem desired and notch the card accordingly. To measure the hem, take the notched card, place it on the edge of the first fold and crease the second turn of the hem the width the notch in the card indicates. Crease for about an inch. Then begin to baste, moving the card a little in advance. Baste the hem as close to the edge as possible so as to catch the first fold.

In hemming, the stitches should be the same distance apart, and each stitch must be made to slant exactly right. To do this hold the work over the first finger of the left hand and put the needle into the work near enough to the hem to touch it (but not under it), and just midway between where it came out for

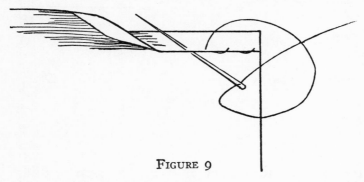

FIGURE 9

the last stitch, and where it is to come out for the next one.   [Fig. 9.]

The needle should be almost on the same line with the hem. Hemming-stitches should not be up and down, nor straight, like running stitches; neither should they be too close together.

The length of the stitch and the length of the space between should be equal.

TUCKING

Tucks are used in many ways; sometimes for shortening the skirts of garments, but more often for ornament.

Always use a notched card to measure with.

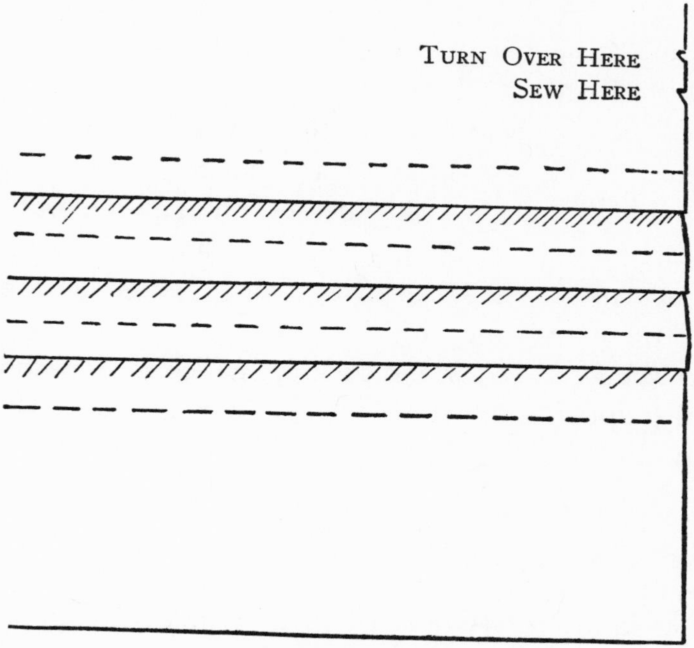

TURN OVER HERE
SEW HERE

FIGURE 10

To make narrow tucks above a hem [Fig. 10] notch the card to indicate the distance from the top of the hem to the line where the sewing will be on the under side of the tuck and from that to the line where the tuck is to be folded. This same measure will do for the other tucks, measuring from the sewing of the last tuck, instead of from the top of the hem.

A tuck covers a space equal to its own depth, and this must be added to the distance desired between the tucks.

Having measured the tuck, double the goods at the line marked for the crease, and baste through the two thicknesses on the line indicated for the sewing. It is basted as it is measured, the measuring card being kept a little in advance of the sewing. A running-stitch is used for the tucking which is done on the upper side of the tuck. As a general rule, tucks should be half their own width apart.

GATHERING

Gathering is done with a double thread on the right side of the material. The rule for ordinary gathering is to take up once and a half as much as is left down. Sew about a quarter of an inch below the edge.

CHAPTER III

BUTTONHOLES AND SCALLOPS

BUTTONHOLES

Buttonholing is a difficult operation for beginners, and it is best to practice on an imaginary opening before making a regular buttonhole. The buttonhole can be marked by drawing a pencil line on the goods and sewed around exactly as for a real buttonhole.

To cut a buttonhole the correct size, lay the button on a paper and make two dots with a pencil on opposite sides of the button. Then fix the gauge of the buttonhole scissors so they will make a cut just a trifle longer than from dot to dot. To be sure it is the right size, slip the button through. Some allowance must be made for what the sewing will take up. This should first be practiced on paper before the material is cut.

Use as coarse a thread and as fine a needle as will go together. As it is very trying to

have the thread give out before the buttonhole is finished, the length of thread is important. For dolly's clothes three-eighths to a
half yard is ample.

The "bar" of the buttonhole is on the inside.
That is, the furthest from the edge of the
garment. Begin by taking three threads across

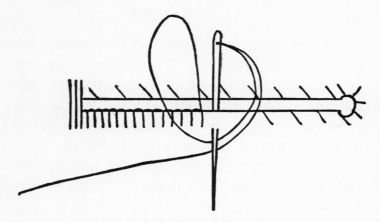

FIGURE II

the end which makes a foundation for the
bar, then overcast the slit. The buttonhole
is held on the first finger of the left hand
and is worked from left to right. Put the
needle in straight, at right angles to the
work. With the thread between the middle fingers, throw back the thread with the

little finger. Put the needle into the buttonhole [Fig. 11], bringing it out on the side
nearer you. Draw it half-way through just
below the line of the overcasting. Take hold of
the thread near enough to the needle to take
the double thickness of thread, and with the
right hand, going from right to left, put the
two threads under the point of the needle, and
pull the needle through. Give a little jerk to
the thread, first toward you, then in the opposite direction. Every stitch is made the
same way and must be exactly the same depth
and should cover the overcasting. Use a cer-
tain thread in the goods as a guide for the depth
of the stitches. Round the corner carefully,
keep the stitches together in the cut, and apart
on the outside, like the sticks of a fan. Turn
and work along the other side to the bar. To
work the bar, put the needle in the cut and
bring it out on the right hand end, and outside of the bar. Hold the buttonhole across
the finger and work the strands of the bar with
the embroidery buttonhole stitch.

The bar should be far enough out so as
just to meet the sewing on the buttonhole. The
ends of the bar should be on a line with the
outside of the buttonhole stitches. When

finished, put the needle through to the wrong side, carrying the thread under three or four of the other threads.

If the buttonhole has been carefully handled, when finished it will be a straight slit, the edges almost meeting. [Fig. 12.]

BUTTON LOOPS

Work from the right side of the material on the edge of the goods. Take three stitches large enough to form a loop to slip over the

FIGURE 12

button; then, without breaking the thread, work over the loop with the embroidery buttonhole stitch. Hold the loop under the left thumb and push the stitches closely together as each one is made. Fasten the threads carefully on the wrong side.

SEWING ON A BUTTON

In sewing on a button, start the thread on the right side so the knot will be hidden by the button. If the button has four holes, the sewing should form a square on the wrong side and a cross on the right side. Use a double thread. After taking the first stitch, slip a pin across the button and sew over it. This permits of sewing the button firmly but not tightly. Another way is, after sewing several times through the holes wrap the stitches between the button and material with the thread two or three times. Then draw through and fasten the thread securely on the wrong side.

HERRINGBONE OR CATCH-STITCH

This stitch is used on the wrong side of the seams of flannel to make them flat. After the seam has been sewed up with a plain running-stitch, open and press as flat as possible. Knot the silk and begin the catch-stitching at the left. Put the needle under the edge of the seam, and draw it through to the top. Take a short running-stitch on one side of the seam near the edge, and then across to the other side, each time advancing a little to the right. By beginning to sew at the left, the thread is crossed at each stitch. The sewing is done of course on the wrong side of the garment.

[Fig. 13.]   On the right side is a double line of running-stitches as nearly as possible invisible.   Herringbone must be perfectly even.

FEATHER-STITCH OR BRIAR-STITCH

Feather-stitching can be used in so many different ways to make garments dainty that I

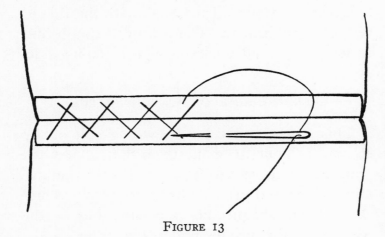

FIGURE 13

am sure every little girl will be amply repaid for learning how to do it well.

This stitch is worked on the right side and toward the person sewing.   The work is held in the left hand over the first finger, and kept in place with the thumb and second finger. The needle being drawn through for the first

stitch, hold the thread firmly under the left
thumb. The second stitch is taken a thread
or two to the left of the central line; and, in
order to form the loop the thread has to be
thrown around from right to left toward you,

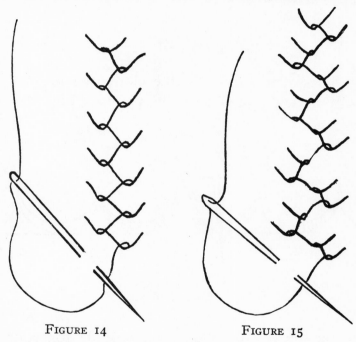

FIGURE 14   FIGURE 15

and then held under the left thumb. The
needle is then brought outside the loop. The
third stitch is again to the right, and so con-
tinue, alternating each time from right to left.
[Fig. 14.]

Double feather-stitching is more elaborate. It is done in exactly the same way as single feather-stitching, except that two stitches are taken each side of the central line instead of one. [Fig. 15.]

SCALLOPS

To scallop, draw on the cloth two lines of half-circles, joined as in the picture [Fig. 16],

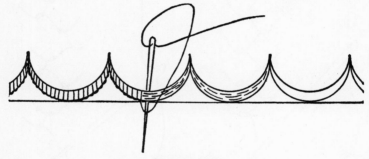

FIGURE 16

using the end of a spool as a guide for your pencil. Fill in with the chain or outline stitch and work with the embroidery button-hole stitch, described on page 28. When finished, cut the material away close to the scallops.

CHAPTER IV

ABOUT THE PATTERNS

Having learned how to do all the stitches both plain and fancy, little girls can now get to work on the pretty patterns. As the purpose of this book is to teach girls how to make their dollies' clothes, all the patterns have been designed simple enough for little fingers to make.

But you see the drawings in the book are too small for any but the tiniest china doll, so you must learn to make them fit all your different-sized dolls.

To do this, patterns should be made first, before cutting into the material. Paper is quite the best thing to practice on, and you can snip away until the patterns are a perfect fit.

To make any one of these patterns for a bigger doll, measure carefully the width of the neck from ear to ear, the length of each shoulder, the distance from the shoulder seam

around the arm to the side seam, the length
of the skirt from under the arm to the knees
or wherever you wish the skirt to end, and
the length of the skirt from the throat to the
bottom of the dress, if there be no yoke, and
from the bottom of the yoke, if there be one.
In measuring for length, allow enough for
a hem as deep as you wish to make it. Also
measure the width of Dolly across the chest,
the length of the arm and the whole measure-
ment around the neck.

Write all these measurements down on a
piece of paper.

Now trace from the book the pattern you
wish to make up. This can be done by putting a thin piece of paper over the drawing.
Put a larger piece of paper on the table in front
of you and make dots on it to correspond with
the measurements of your doll.

For instance, if you have a twenty-four-inch
doll make two dots about the center of the
paper, but up toward the top, for half the
neck. These should be three inches apart.
Then, on a slanting line, make another dot
three inches away for the shoulder. About
an inch and a half below that but a little be-
yond—to the outside—make another dot for

the distance around the arm, and in a slanting line down from it put a dot twelve inches away. Now from the center of the neck measure down fifteen inches and put a dot for the length of the skirt. This allows for the hem. Put the central dots of the lines around the arm, the width of the doll's chest apart.

Now about the center of these dots place your traced pattern and draw lines from dot to dot as nearly corresponding as possible with the shape of the little pattern. Of course there may be some mistakes, but that does not make much difference, as only paper is being used.

When the pattern is cut out hold it to the doll and see if it nearly fits; then cut the other parts in the same way. It is better to have the patterns a little bigger than wanted as they can be taken in to fit. Before making up in the nice material, try cutting out the patterns from a piece of old muslin or cheese cloth, and basting them together to see how nearly they fit.

In cutting a neck or around an arm do not make the curves too big until the pattern is tried on, as it is much easier to cut it out than to add to it.

Every pattern in the book can be cut in some

such way, or if you do not want to take all the trouble to measure each part you can just make dots for the neck and the length, and with the little traced sketch in the middle, draw a big pattern like it. Then hold it to the doll and cut off what is left over.

After the patterns are made put the material on a table and pin the pattern to it by pins at the neck, each shoulder, on the under-arm seams and at the bottom, so it will not slip. With your largest scissors cut all around the edges of the pattern without lifting the material from the table. Where pattern is marked "Fold," put it on a fold of stuff.

In making up the patterns join the pieces together, taking care that the notches come opposite each other. Baste neatly and try on to see that it fits before sewing.

CHAPTER V
THE INFANT'S OUTFIT

The first full-page picture [Fig. 17] shows

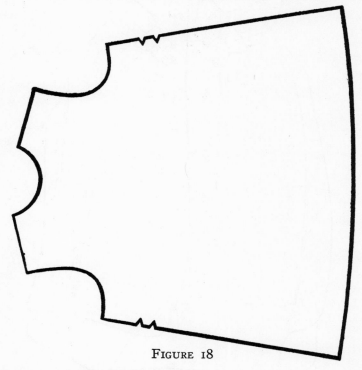

FIGURE 18

us the infant dolly dressed for a ride in her coach. Cut the coat from any soft, white

INFANT'S OUTFIT—FIGURE 17

woolen material or from China silk or
piqué.

Be sure the material is folded together in a
straight line, lengthwise, before the pattern for
the back is placed on it; and see that in cut-

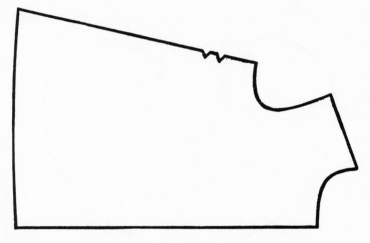

FIGURE 19

ting all the parts the material is not twisted.
This holds good for all pattern cutting.

Pin the back [Fig. 18] to the front [Fig. 19]
according to the notches. Baste before sewing.
Do the long seams first and then the shoulders. Turn back the fronts for hems and hem
them so neatly that the stitches do not show
through. Fasten with three pearl buttons and

buttonholes. The bottom should be turned up two inches in a hem.

The capes [Fig. 20] and sleeves [Fig. 21] should be lined with silk. Lining makes the capes look prettier and if in the sleeves the coat will slip on more easily.

To line the capes cut the silk and outside ex-

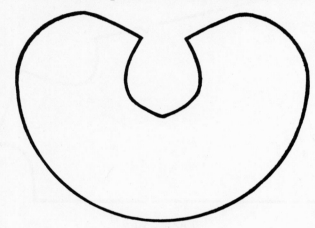

FIGURE 20

actly the same size and sew on the wrong side in a narrow seam. Then turn over and baste the edges flat on the right side. Either press it with an iron or stitch it on the machine several times for a trimming.

Join the sleeves at the notches and sew up the seams. Make the silk lining in the same way and baste the two together, wrong side to wrong side.   Gather around the top and bottom.   Sew the hand gathers into a straight stitched band for the cuff.   Pin the gathers to the right side of the band, baste, sew, and remove the basting.   Fold over the band to the wrong side, turn in the edge and hem down.

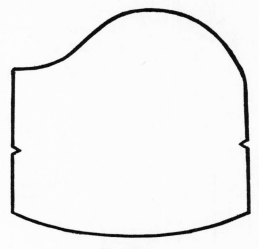

FIGURE 21

The cuff should later be stitched on the machine to make a pretty finish.

In putting in a sleeve hold the wrong side of the coat toward you with the sleeve through the armhole underneath.   Put the seam of the sleeve a little to the front of the under-arm seam and arrange most of the gathers to the

INFANT'S LONG DRESS—FIGURE 22

top.   Baste and sew.   Finish the edges of the
seams with a bias piece of silk for a binding.

Fit the capes carefully to the neck of the
coat, taking care not to stretch it.   Turn down
the seams on the wrong side and sew over
them a narrow facing of silk, so they lie flat
to the coat.

The dress [Fig. 22] should be made of fine
lawn or soft nainsook.   The back and front
are cut alike, and the pattern should be placed
on a lengthwise fold of the material.   Join
the skirt [Fig. 23] according to the notches.
Slash down the center of the back a little way
to form an opening, and turn back and hem
each side.

The bottom of the skirt may be turned up
into a plain hem two inches deep, or it may
have three or five fine tucks above the hem.
In this case the skirt must be cut longer to
allow for them.

Gather the top of the skirt with small stitches
in a narrow seam and join it to the yoke
[Fig. 24].   This can be done in two ways.
Either turn the right side of the yoke down
on the right side of the skirt, and sew in a
narrow seam, which is later bound on the
wrong side; or the wrong side of skirt and

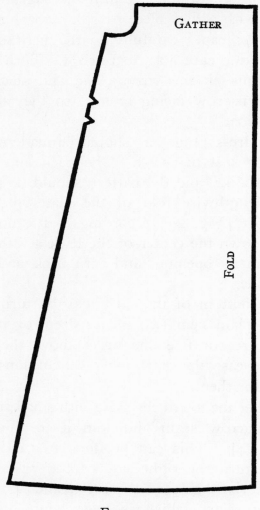

FIGURE 23

yoke may be sewed together and the seam
turned up on the yoke on the right side and
covered with beading or a narrow bias band of
the material, which is then briar-stitched.

The yoke is cut without a shoulder seam and
is hemmed at the back where it is fastened
with tiny buttons and buttonholes.

Join the sleeves [Fig. 25] according to the

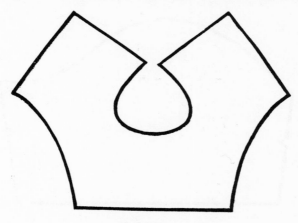

FIGURE 24

notches and gather into the armhole, finishing
with a narrow binding. The gathers at the
wrist are sewed into a narrow beading instead
of a cuff. This should be just the width of
Dolly's arm and should be finished on the edge
with a narrow frill of lace. The lace should
be held loosely over the first finger of the left

hand and overhanded in tiny stitches to the beading. Always hold the lace toward you, with the seam up, and the right side turned to the right side of the material. When the whipping, or overhanding, is done, open the seam and press it flat with the nail.

The narrowest French Valenciennes lace should be used as it is daintiest for infants'

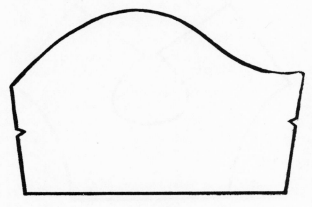

FIGURE 25

clothes. The neck should also be finished with beading and a lace ruffle. Ribbon is run through neck and sleeves. Finish the yoke and the bottom of the hem with briar-stitching.

Cut the long white petticoat [Fig. 26] from fine nainsook with a lawn ruffle. The back and **front** [Fig. 27] are cut alike. Join the skirt

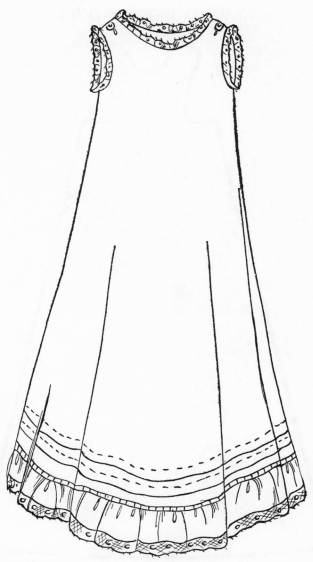

Infant's Long White Petticoat—Figure 26

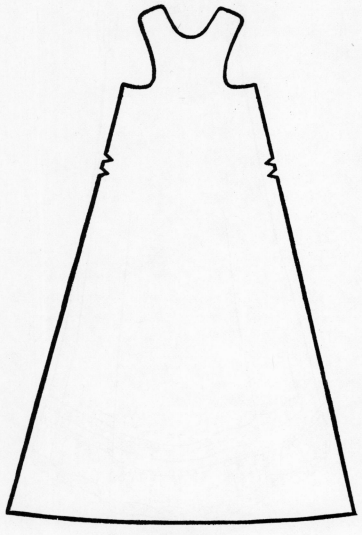

FIGURE 27

by the under-arm seams according to the notches; then baste and sew in a felled seam.

The bottom of the skirt may be hemmed or it may have a ruffle at the bottom. This should be cut across the material and be once and a half as wide as the bottom of the skirt. The seams of the ruffle are joined with the tiniest French seam, or the selvages can be overhanded if they are not heavy. Sew this ruffle to the skirt on the right side and cover the seam with narrow insertion or beading.

The skirt is not sewed on the shoulders but is joined by buttons and buttonholes. The front shoulder pieces lap over the back. Cutting the skirt in this way makes it much easier to dress Dolly, as the skirt is slipped over the head. Overhand the neck and armholes with lace, also the ruffle at the bottom of the skirt. Three hand-run tucks just above the ruffle add a very dainty touch to this little garment.

The flannel skirt [Fig. 28] is cut from a straight piece of fine white flannel, joined in a seam at the back, leaving an opening at the top for a vent. Open the seam and work with herringbone. Turn up at the lower end for an inch-wide hem, which should be briarstitched. Or the bottom of the hem may be

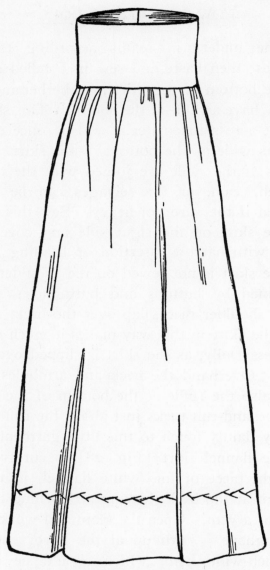

INFANT'S FLANNEL SKIRT—FIGURE 28

marked with a scallop and buttonholed in white embroidery silk.

The skirt [Fig. 29] is then gathered into a wide muslin band [Fig. 30] large enough to fit around Dolly's body. Lap over at the back and fasten with two tiny safety pins.

The cap may be made in two ways. The one pictured [Fig. 17] is very simple, and suitable for an infant or very small doll. Measure across the top of Dolly's head from ear to ear, and cut two pieces of insertion the exact length. Sew these together. Then gather along the edge of one piece and draw into a knot to form the back. Sew beading all around the cap and run ribbon through the beading. Finish with two ribbon rosettes, one on either temple, and ribbon ties.

The rosettes may be made from short ends of ribbon knotted in the middle and the ends then sewed to a tiny circle of canvas or buckram.

A pattern [Fig. 31] is given for another cap which is suitable for a medium-sized doll. Cut from lawn, making the front edge big enough to go around the doll's head. Join the front piece according to the notches and sew in the round piece at the back in a tiny

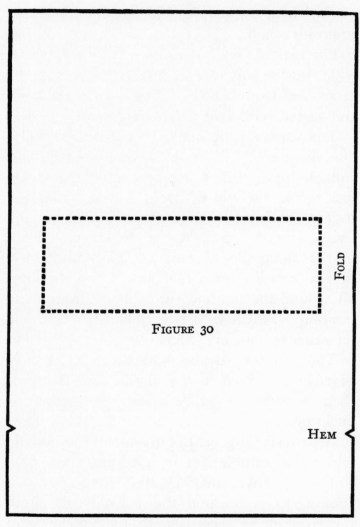

FIGURE 30

FOLD

HEM

FIGURE 29

seam.   Edge with insertion and a frill of lace
around the face.   A stiff standing bow of ribbon adorns the top.

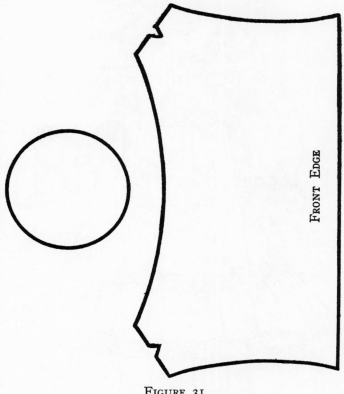

FRONT EDGE

FIGURE 31

Little bootees are worn with this costume;
but it is better to buy them.   They cost but a
few cents in the shops.

PARTY DRESS—FIGURE 32

CHAPTER VI

THE PARTY DRESS

This dainty dress [Fig. 32] may be just as elaborate as possible. The more lace and insertion used the fluffier and prettier it will look. Cut like the pattern shown in Fig. 23. Join the skirt according to the notches and gather to the yoke [Fig. 24]. This yoke is also made without a shoulder seam because it is simpler and more easily trimmed. Close the sleeves [Fig. 25] according to the notches and gather into the armhole. Gather the lower edge to insertion and finish with a frill of lace. Run ribbon under the insertion, or if beading is used instead, through it. Bows of ribbon adorn the yoke.

The skirt may have one or two rows of insertion running around it, at the bottom, a lace-edged ruffle. The insertion is sewed to the right side of the skirt and yoke. The edges may be stitched on the machine and the material cut away underneath, except a tiny edge

which is turned back and stitched again.   Or it
can be sewed on the right side by hand stitch-
ing, the material cut away and the edges overhanded with tiny stitches.   This dress is dainty
when made of dotted swiss, or French muslin.

The underclothes to go with it [Figs. 33
and 34] are made of fine lawn.   The little

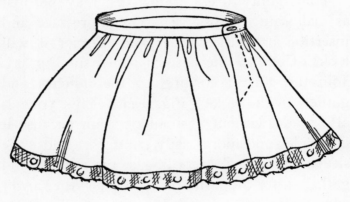

FIGURE 33

skirt is cut from a straight piece sewed together at the back and gathered to a narrow
band fastened with a button and buttonhole.
Trim with a ruffle of two-inch-wide German
Valenciennes lace, overhanded to the edge.
Often lace, instead of being gathered for a
ruffle, has the upper thread in its edge pulled,
which shirrs it to any desired fulness.   Another

ruffle may be sewed to the skirt above this one, as the more beruffled the petticoat the more the skirt stands out.

The undergarment [Fig. 34] is simple and easily made, for the little waist and panties

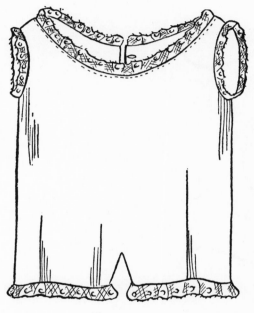

FIGURE 34

[Fig. 35] are cut in one piece. In cutting this pattern for a larger doll, the slash will have to be made as long as the legs, from the knee up. Join the shoulder seams and slashed parts to form the legs. Turn in the backs from the

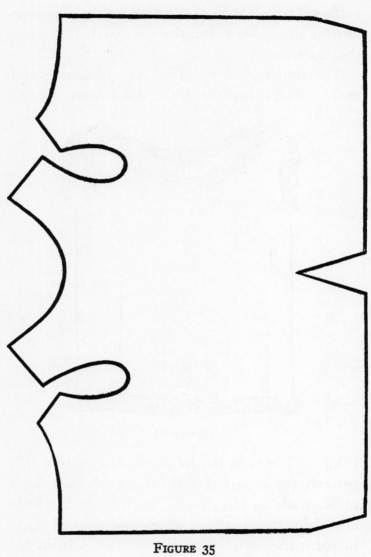

FIGURE 35

tops of the slashes for hems and fasten with
buttons and buttonholes.   Face the armholes,
neck and panty legs with a narrow facing and

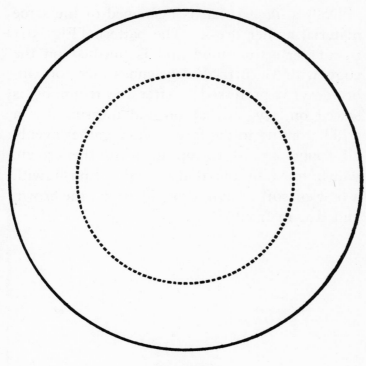

FIGURE 36

finish with a frill of lace; wider for the legs
and quite tiny for the rest.

To this outfit may be added a flannel petticoat made exactly like the white one, only

finished with a briar-stitched hem. This completes Dolly's *lingerie*.

White slippers and socks should be worn with this dress.

Dolly's *lingerie* hat is fashioned of the same material as her dress. The pattern [Fig. 36] is cut perfectly round and is finished on the edge with German Valenciennes lace, or embroidery, if preferred. After the trimming is sewed on, try the hat on and measure for a frill becoming to the face. Next, gather evenly all round and draw up to form the crown, which must fit the doll's head. Finish with a bow of soft ribbon, brought round the crown and tied in front.

CHAPTER VII

DOLLY'S STREET CLOTHES

Here is Dolly dressed for a walk. Her coat may be made from any desired material. If for a very dressy one, cut from velvet or heavy silk. Serge or thin broadcloth, trimmed with braid and small fancy buttons, makes a smart little coat. Of the wash materials, flannel and piqué are perhaps the favorites.

The one here pictured [Fig. 37] is made from piqué and cut from the same pattern used for Fig. 17, only shortened so as to come a few inches above the short skirt. Be sure in cutting the pattern [Figs. 18 and 19] to lay it lengthwise of the material, especially in silk or flannel, and if stripes are to be used join them before laying the two sides of the pattern on the material, so they will match when sewed.

Join the under-arm and shoulder seams in a felled seam. Turn back the fronts for a

DOLLY'S STREET COSTUME—FIGURE 37

facing and the lower edge for a hem. Make
the sleeves and either plait or gather them into
the armhole binding with a narrow piece of
silk, if the material be heavy. Join the deep
collar to the neck, without a band, and bind
the inside rough edges, or face them flat to
the coat.

Fasten down the front with pearl buttons.
The buttons may also trim the sleeves. The
collar can be made a little more fancy by binding the edge with a color or sewing lace or
embroidery around the edge.

In such a tiny coat it is difficult to make
real pockets, but they may be simulated by
sewing little stitched flaps to either side.
Black shoes and white stockings look well with
this coat and hat. The hat is a simple straw
trimmed with a band of ribbon with long loops
and ends down the back. Little girls who
know how to do raffia work can easily make
such a hat for themselves.

DOLLY'S EVERYDAY DRESS—FIGURE 38

CHAPTER VIII

THE EVERYDAY DRESS

This little dress [Fig. 38] is plain and easily made. In colored lawn, gingham or chambray it will look very well. Lay the material in box plaits before cutting out—three plaits for the front and two for the back. To make these plaits fold the middle one down a lengthwise crease of the material, measuring as if for a deep tuck. Then make another tuck on either side, being very accurate as to measuring and allowing the proper space between when the tucks are opened out. End the plaits a little below the waist line. Sew the tucks firmly, then press them open, being careful that the middle of each plait runs on the line of the sewing and does not twist. Baste and press flat.

Be careful in pinning the pattern to have the center of the front pattern [Fig. 39] in the middle of the center plait. Cut out the back [Fig. 40] so a box plait comes on either side

of the center.   Make an opening at the back
of the neck and face back with a narrow strip
of the material.   Join the front and back according to the notches; make French seams.

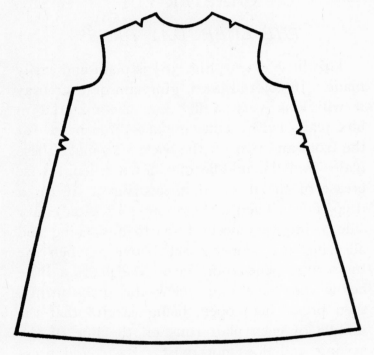

FIGURE 39

Turn up the lower edge and hem neatly, or
briar-stitch.

Join the sleeves [Fig. 41] and gather into
the armhole. Gather lower edge of sleeve to

form a ruffle, and edge with lace or embroidery.
Make the neck in like manner. As these
gatherings are not sewed into a band they must
be stayed or made firm by sewing them to a

FIGURE 40

narrow strip of the material or tape underneath.

The belt is a straight piece of the material,
doubled over lengthwise, with the edges turned

in and stitched on the outside. One end should
be folded into a point. The belt is run through
strips of the material sewed to the dress on

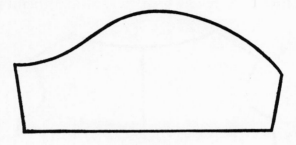

FIGURE 41

the under-arm seams at the waist line. The belt
is buttoned in front.

Underwear for this dress is made from the
same patterns as the preceding ones, only not
so elaborately.

CHAPTER IX

DOLLY'S APRON

This dainty apron [Fig. 42] is worn over any plain dress. It is made of lawn or dimity or of checked gingham. To cut it, fold over the material on a lengthwise crease and put the pattern [Fig. 43] with the front edge so it comes on the fold of the material.

Join the shoulder seams in a flat fell and hem the backs for buttons and buttonholes. Either gather or plait the long, straight piece in the front, into a space wide enough to fit over Dolly's chest. Bind it with a narrow piece of the material to hold it firm. If plaits are used instead of gathers, fold half of them to the right and half to the left so they face on each side toward the center. Hem the arm-holes.

Finish around the square neck with embroidery insertion, turning in the edges on each side. Put an edging to match around the bottom. sewing it on flat and not in a ruffle. If

DOLLY'S APRON—FIGURE 42

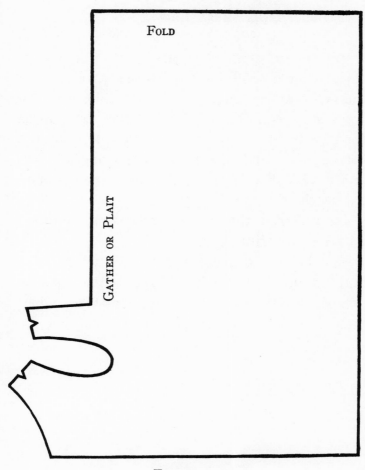

FIGURE 43

preferred, a tiny edge of lace can be whipped to either edge of the insertion around the neck, to make a more fancy finish.

Another pretty way to make this apron would be to trim the neck with a band of colored lawn or linen, and to put on a hem of the color at the bottom. To do this, sew the seam so it comes on the right side, turn in as for a hem, and sew on the right side. Or the hem can be stitched across the bottom in color, and a plain band put on the neck and stitched to match.

If preferred, the apron may be just hemmed without any trimming.

Be careful to measure the spaces for the buttons and buttonholes so they come exactly opposite, else the apron will pucker when fastened.

CHAPTER X

DOLLY'S NIGHTGOWN

Here is Dolly ready for bed [Fig. 44]. One half of the nightie pattern is shown

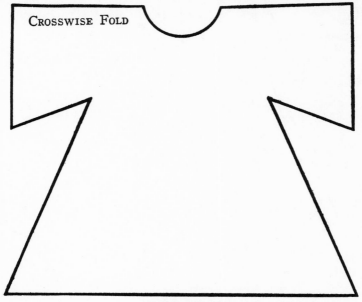

FIGURE 45

[Fig. 45]. To cut it fold the material over crosswise instead of lengthwise, as in all the

DOLLY READY FOR BED—FIGURE 44

other patterns. It should be made of nain-sook or lawn. As this little garment slips on over the head, the neck opening should be amply large, but not too large. If it gets too big by mistake, a beading may be run around the edge and the lace sewed to that; then it can be drawn up with baby ribbon.

Join the side seams according to the notches and make a felled seam. Trim the low neck and sleeves with Valenciennes lace. Hem the lower edge and the nightdress is made.

To make the nightdress very fine, short strips of insertion may be sewed down from the neck in front. Sew flat as was described before and then cut away the material beneath.

DOLLY'S KIMONO—FIGURE 46

CHAPTER XI

DOLLY'S KIMONO

This comfortable little kimono [Fig. 46] is made very much the same as the nightie, except that it is open down the front as is shown in Fig. 47. In cutting the pattern, fold over the material as for the nightie; but instead of just cutting the neck opening on the front fold, open the front by following the dotted lines on each side. If you want your kimono to lap over on the fronts, instead of making the lines apart, as shown in the dots of the pattern, cut the front piece directly up the center until Dolly's neck is reached, when two sloping lines may be made to the shoulders.

Sew up both the under-arm seams and the under parts of the sleeves. Turn up the hem for the bottom and bind the sleeves and each side of the front with broad bands of some contrasting plain color. This binding is put on by sewing the right side of the silk to the wrong side of the kimono; baste it carefully

79

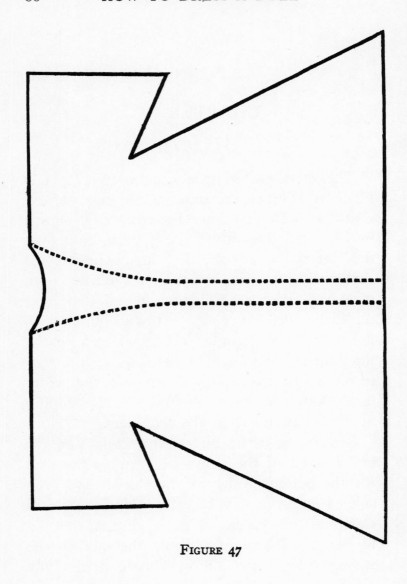

FIGURE 47

first, then turn over on to the right side, press down the seam and baste along the outer edge. Then measure the binding carefully with a notched measuring card, to get it exactly even. Turn in a little of the edge as for a hem. Baste again, and either hem neatly or stitch it on the machine. Cut the silk for the binding on the straight of the weave.

If ribbon is used instead of material for this binding, the edge of it should be sewed to the wrong side of the kimono, with the edge of the ribbon pointing toward the sleeve. It is stitched through but not so as to show on the right side, then is turned over the edge and basted and sewed on the right side.

This kimono may be made of any soft, woolen stuff, or of silk or flowered lawn. Pieces of silk from mother's party frocks would be lovely to use. If the material of the kimono is figured, the binding should be plain and in a contrasting color. If the kimono is plain, pretty flowered ribbon, silks or lawn should be used.

A plain band may be trimmed by briar-stitching down each side, or one may stitch the edge on the machine with another line of stitches about a quarter of an inch apart.

RED RIDING HOOD COSTUME—FIGURE 48

CHAPTER XII

THE RED RIDING HOOD COSTUME

The chief feature of Red Riding Hood's costume [Fig. 48] is her cape. Almost any kind of red woolen or silk material will make up nicely, and the cape can be finished in several ways. It may be hemmed all around and left plain; it may be lined throughout, though this is not necessary and makes extra work; or it may be faced back with a band of red silk. The outside may be feather-stitched instead of hemmed, and may be trimmed with several rows of narrow soutache braid.

In cutting the cape [Fig. 49] fold over the material lengthwise; put the edge marked "Fold" on the fold of the material and cut carefully on the circular lines. If the cape is lined, it is basted and sewed to the material, right side to right side, leaving an opening at the top to turn it. Turn in the silk and the wool at the neck and stitch together close

83

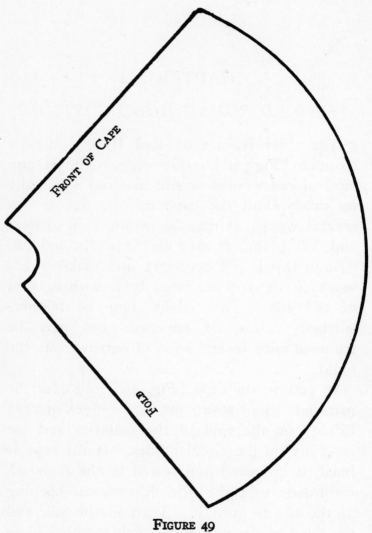

FRONT OF CAPE

FOLD

FIGURE 49

to the edge on the right side. If the cape is lined it is simply overhanded to the hood as neatly as possible; if unlined it is sewed in a seam and the rough edges bound.

Cut the hood the shape of the pattern [Fig. 50], making it plenty large enough to

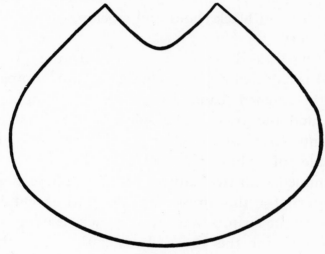

FIGURE 50

slip on easily over Dolly's head and make a becoming frill. It is lined with silk the same shade, in the way described for the cape. After lining, run a casing a short distance from the outer edge, for a drawing-string. This casing is a narrow piece of ribbon or bias silk sewed on both edges. The ends are left open for the ribbon to be run in, to draw up the hood into a ruffle.

Fasten the hood to the cape without a neck-band in the way described. The cape must reach almost to the hem of the dress.

This cape may be worn over any kind of frock that is rather plain. Simple under-clothes and black shoes and stockings complete the outfit.

The little dress shown in the picture [Fig. 48] is a dotted red and white gingham trimmed with stitched bands of plain red gingham around the yoke. The side pieces are cut in points front and back and the little yoke is made of white embroidery. The skirt is trimmed with two half-inch tucks. There is no pattern for this dress, but the skirt is cut in a straight strip, sewed up the back, leaving an opening for the vent. It is gathered at the waistline to form a simple baby waist.

CHAPTER XIII

A PIERROT COSTUME

The Pierrot, or clown, suit here pictured [Fig. 51] is one of the most attractive as well as the most easily made of all the fancy dresses for dolls. This one is made of white satin and trimmed with black velvet buttons, but it can be made up in very cheap materials of gaudy colorings. One leg and sleeve may be made of a color contrasting with the other leg and sleeve, as red and green, orange and black, blue and yellow.

Cut two pieces according to the pattern [Fig. 52]. The dotted line under the arms should be placed on the straight of the goods, which brings a bias seam down the front. The back is left open and hemmed for buttons and buttonholes, as the buttons in front are not used for fastening, but only for ornament.

Sew the lower part of each half up as far as the notches to form the legs. These legs are then turned up and gathered a little above

PIERROT, OR CLOWN, SUIT—FIGURE 51

the lower edge to form a ruffle.   The sleeve-
ruffle is finished in the same way.   Both should
be stayed with narrow bands underneath.   Or

FIGURE 52

narrow casings can be made and pieces of
elastic run through them.

The sleeves [Fig. 53] are joined according

to the notches, gathered in the armhole and
finished at the edge like the trousers.   A
straight piece of material, folded double and
gathered as full as possible forms the ruff
around the neck.   The ruff is gathered to the

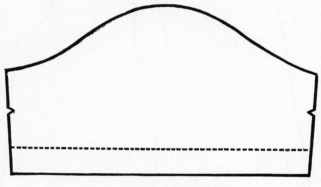

FIGURE 53

neck and the edges are bound and hemmed
down flat to the suit.   This neck-ruff is a very
important feature of the suit and should always
be white.   Three or even four times the meas-
urement of the neck should be allowed for it
so as to make it very frilly.

Cut three pieces like the cap pattern [Fig.
54], one of satin, another of crinoline or canvas for stiffening, and a third of thin silk or
lawn for lining.   Cover the crinoline with the
satin and face with the lining.   Hem the edges

all round.   The cap must be sewed up on the
outside, so join according to the notches and
overhand with very small stitches.   Trim with
large velvet buttons.   If the overhanding cannot be very neatly done the stitches may be

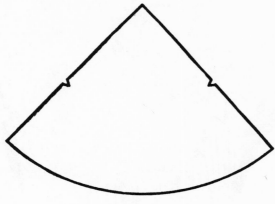

FIGURE 54

covered by sewing over them a line of gold
braid.

White silk stockings and white slippers
ornamented with black velvet buttons complete
this stunning costume.

Underclothes are entirely dispensed with.

JAPANESE DRESS—FIGURE 55

CHAPTER XIV

A JAPANESE DRESS

This Japanese dress [Fig. 55] is exactly like the ones the little ladies wear in far Japan. Cut the pattern [Fig. 56] from bright colored silk or cotton stuff. If you can get some of the real Japanese silks it will be much prettier.

In cutting this pattern the material is folded crosswise as for the kimono, and the fronts are cut according to the dotted lines or in a straight line down the middle, as described in making the kimono. The facing is put down the front in the same way, too. These facings may be of plain silk or cotton, carrying out the chief color of the dress.

The sleeves [Fig. 57] are straight pieces of the material lined with the plain. In cutting them, double over the material so it runs the same way as the body of the dress, put the end marked "Fold" on the crease and cut with the notches as in the pattern. Sew the ends together.

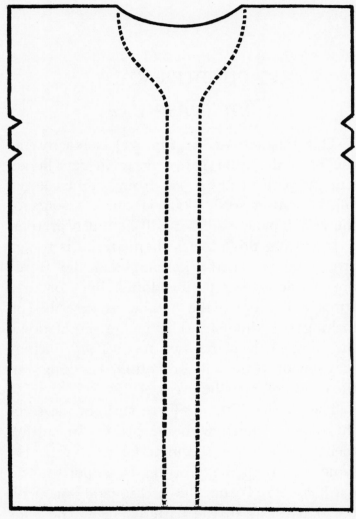

FIGURE 56

Now sew up the sides of the dress to the notches; and above the notches sew in the sleeves, fitting the notches of one to the notches of the other. This will leave the loose sleeve-ends hanging free.

The dress is completed by a wide sash tied

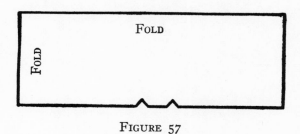

FIGURE 57

in a stiff bow at the back. Make the sash of a strip of the same material as the facing and hem so as not to have raw edges.

The bottom of the dress is turned up and hemmed neatly.

THE END